T0070550

MUSIC MINUS ONE CLARINET

ANDRÉ HAJDU

אנד̄רה היידו

JEWISH RHAPSODY

(TRUAT MELEKH)

FOR B-FLAT CLARINET/BASS CLARINET
AND STRING ORCHESTRA

תרועת מלך

רפסודיה יהודית לקלרנית ולתזמורת כלי קשת

3246

SUGGESTIONS FOR USING THIS MMO EDITION

WE HAVE TRIED to create a product that will provide you an easy way to learn and perform a concerto with a full orchestra in the comfort of your own home. Because it involves a fixed orchestral performance, there is an inherent lack of flexibility in tempo and cadenza length. The following MMO features and techniques will reduce these inflexibilities and help you maximize the effectiveness of the MMO practice and performance system:

Where the soloist begins a movement *solo*, we have provided an introductory measure with subtle taps inserted at the actual tempo before the soloist's entrance.

Chapter stops on your CD are conveniently located throughout the piece at the beginnings of practice sections, and are cross-referenced in the score. This should help you quickly find a desired place in the music as you learn the piece.

Chapter stops have also been placed at orchestra entrances (after cadenzas, for example) so that, with the help of a second person, it is possible to perform a seamless version of the concerto alongside your MMO CD accompaniment. While we have allotted what is generally considered an average amount of time for a cadenza, each performer will have a different interpretation and observe individ-

ual tempi. Your personal rendition may preclude a perfect "fit" within the space provided. Therefore, by having a second person press the pause ❚❚ button on your CD player after the start of each cadenza, followed by the next track ▶▶❙ button, your CD will be cued to the orchestra's re-entry. When you as soloist are at the end of the cadenza or other solo passage, the second person can press the play ▶ (or pause ❚❚ button) on the CD remote to allow a synchronized orchestra re-entry.

Regarding tempi: again, we have observed generally accepted tempi, but some may wish to perform at a different tempo, or to slow down or speed up the accompaniment for practice purposes. You can purchase from MMO (or from other audio and electronics dealers) specialized CD players which allow variable speed while maintaining proper pitch. This is an indispensable tool for the serious musician and you may wish to look into purchasing this useful piece of equipment for full enjoyment of all your MMO editions.

We want to provide you with the most useful practice and performance accompaniments possible. If you have any suggestions for improving the MMO system, please feel free to contact us. You can reach us by e-mail at mmomus@aol.com.

Music Minus One

3246

André Hajdu
Jewish Rhapsody
for B-flat Clarinet/Bass Clarinet and Orchestra

T0033876

°2001 MMO Music Group, Inc. All rights reserved.
JEWISH RHAPSODY °1975 by IMI/Israel Music Institute, P.O.Box 3004, IL-61030 Tel Aviv, Israel.
Used by permission of the publisher.
Orchestral parts may be hired internationally by inquiring at the above address
(Tel. 972.3.5246475 and 5245275; facsimile 972.3.5245276)
In the USA, Canada & Mexico contact the Theodore Presser Co. rental department, 588 North Gulph Road,
King of Prussia, PA 19406
(Tel. 610.525.3636 ext. 225 or 227; facsimile 610.527.7841)

4

Jewish Rhapsody
(Truat Melekh)
FOR B-FLAT CLARINET/BASS CLARINET
AND STRING ORCHESTRA

תרועת מלך

רפסודיה יהודית לקלרנית ולתזמורת כלי קשת

KOL NIDREY   I   כל נדרי

ANDRÉ HAJDU
אנדרה היידו
composed 1974

(Four quarter-note taps precede clarinet entrance)

↓ 1 19 44
Rubato, lento
semplice

B.Cl.

pp

↓ 2 20

A [Allegro moderato]   [poco accel.]   [rit.]

p

↓ 3 21

B   [meno mosso]

mf

p

↓ 4 22

C   [poco rit.]

mp

* ∧ = longer
ν = shorter

MMO 3246

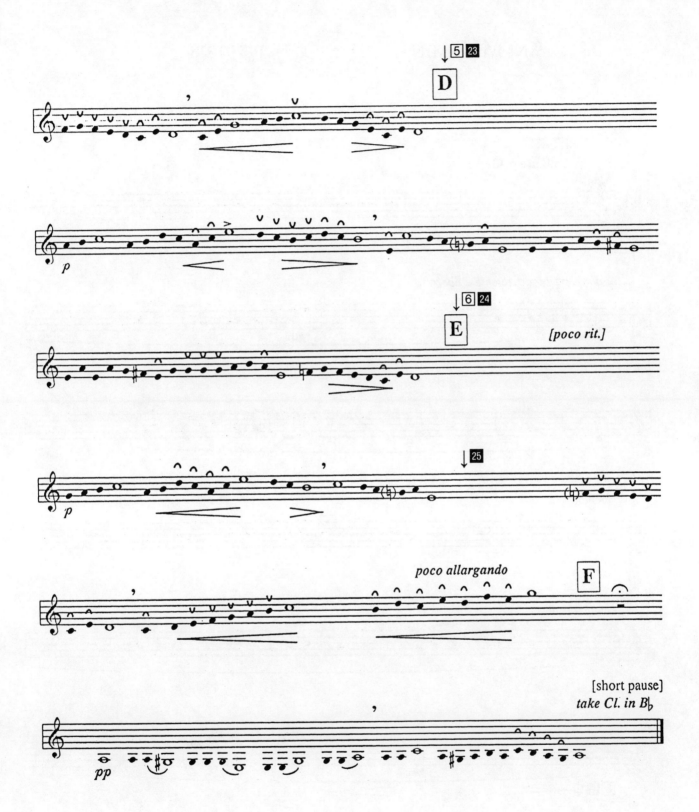

ANI MA'AMIN II אני מאמין

* - three ways blowing the shofar on Rosh ha'Shana (Jewish new year)

Niggun and Shofar III רפושו ווגיני

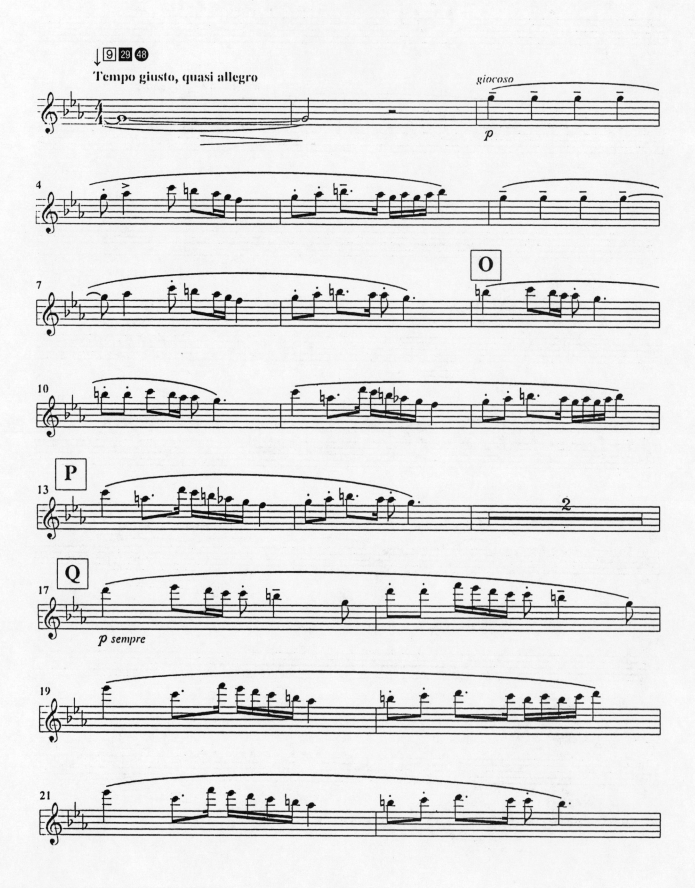

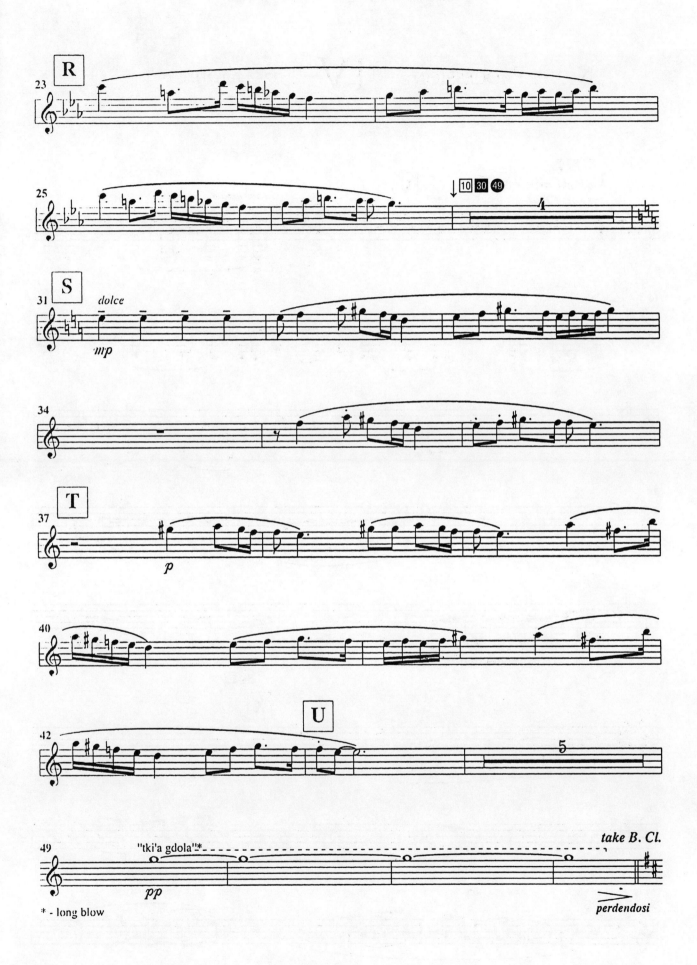

* - long blow

NIGHT PROCESSION IV תהלוכת לילה

DANCES FROM ABU'S COURTYARD

V

ריקודים מחצר עבו

PRAYER VI תפילה

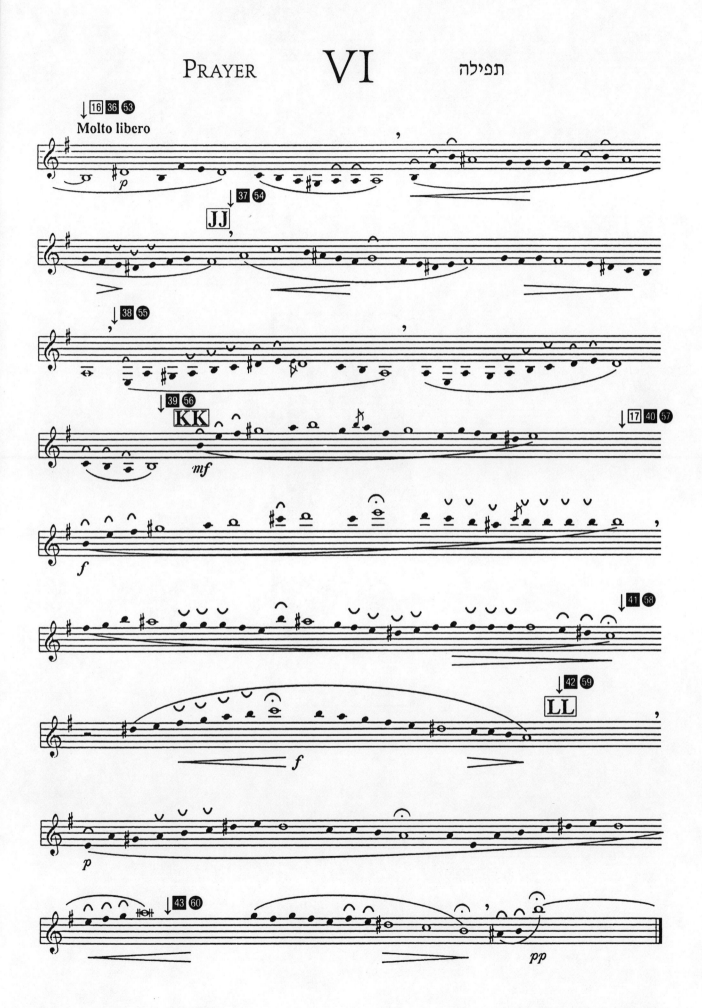

MUSIC MINUS ONE
50 Executive Boulevard
Elmsford, New York 10523-1325
800-669-7464 (U.S.)/914-592-1188 (International)

www.musicminusone.com
e-mail: mmogroup@musicminusone.com